The 7 Day Keto Jump Start Plan:

The Best Recipes for Easy Weight Loss in 7 Days

By Adam Pembroke

FREE BONUS GIFT:

The 30 Day Low Carb Diet Ketosis Plan

Thank you so much for purchasing this book!

As a thank you, and to get our relationship started right, I'd love to offer you're a **free** copy of "The 30 Day Low Car Diet Ketosis Plan."

This bonus picks up where this book leaves off and will help further guide you through an entire month of your weigh loss journey.

I am offering this because I think it's an excellent complement tc this book, and because I want to see you succeed and reach your health goals.

Get your free ebook bonus right here.

© **Copyright 2015 by FTS Media Group - All rights reserved.**

This document is geared towards providing exact and reliable information in regards to the topic and issue covered. The publication is sold with the idea that the publisher is not required to render accounting, officially permitted, or otherwise, qualified services. If advice is necessary, legal or professional, a practiced individual in the profession should be ordered.

This book is not intended as a substitute for the medical advice of physicians. The reader should regularly consult a physician in matters relating to his/her health and particularly with respect to any symptoms that may require diagnosis or medical attention.

From a Declaration of Principles which was accepted and approved equally by a Committee of the American Bar Association and a Committee of Publishers and Associations.

In no way is it legal to reproduce, duplicate, or transmit any part of this document in either electronic means or in printed format. Recording of this publication is strictly prohibited and any storage of this document is not allowed unless with written permission from the publisher. All rights reserved.

The information provided herein is stated to be truthful and consistent, in that any liability, in terms of inattention or otherwise, by any usage or abuse of any policies, processes, or directions contained within is the solitary and utter responsibility of the recipient reader. Under no circumstances will any legal responsibility or blame be held against the publisher for any reparation, damages, or monetary loss due to the information herein, either directly or indirectly.

Respective authors own all copyrights not held by the publisher.

The information herein is offered for informational purposes solely, and is universal as so. The presentation of the information is without contract or any type of guarantee assurance.

The trademarks that are used are without any consent, and the publication of the trademark is without permission or backing by the trademark owner. All trademarks and brands within this book are for clarifying purposes only and are the owned by the owners themselves, not affiliated with this document.

TABLE OF CONTENTS

INTRODUCTION

CHAPTER 1: The Ketogenic Diet and the Science Behind It

CHAPTER 2: The Benefits of Going on a Ketogenic Diet

CHAPTER 3: How to Make Your Transition to the Ketogenic Diet Go as Smoothly as Possible

CHAPTER 4: 1 Week Ketogenic Meal Plan #1

CHAPTER 5: 1 Week Ketogenic Meal Plan #2

CHAPTER 6: 1 Week Ketogenic Meal Plan #3

CHAPTER 7: The Importance of Proper Hydration

CHAPTER 8: Transitioning off a Keto Diet to Long Term Healthy Eating

CHAPTER 9: Top Ten Tips for Staying on a Keto Diet

CHAPTER 10: Conclusion/Final Words

Introduction

Jump start your Ketogenic diet with this simple and easy 7 day weight loss plan. If you are new to the concept, then you might be thinking that the word 'ketogenic' sounds like something you would have heard during 6th grade science class. But don't let the fancy words put your off, the Keto diet is simple to understand and even easier to follow. Plus the results people have been achieving on this diet have the world wanting to know more! So this guide is going to tell you everything you need to know as well as provide you with an easy plan to get started. So let's jump to it!

To put it simply, the aim of the Ketogenic diet is to put the body into a state of ketosis, where it is breaking down fat and using it as the main energy source. This is achieved by eating more fats and less carbs. Sounds like a contradiction, doesn't it? But we are talking about the good kind of fats like olive oil, avocado and nuts. With an increase in fats and proteins and a decrease in carbohydrates the body starts to take energy from ketones (fats) rather than from glucose (carbs). This jump starts the metabolism putting it into a crazy fast pace helping us to lose weight and get lean!

There are many benefits to starting the Keto diet. Here are just a few to wet your appetite:

- Hunger suppressant
- Weight loss enhancer
- Energy booster
- Disease prevention

With any new diet there are some health considerations to take into account before starting. If you have any concerns or previous health conditions, please consult you doctor before starting the Ketogenic diet. Those who have diabetes, kidney or heart problems should take special care. The increased fat and protein levels may put strain on these organs. Remember also that doctors are not diet specialists so consider additionally seeing a qualified dietician.

The 7 Day Keto Jump Start Plan will be your eyes and ears into the Keto diet. Here's a sneak peak into what you are going to learn throughout this book. Firstly you are going to learn all about how the diet works and the science behind it. Secondly we will inform you on all the benefits of this type of diet. Thirdly we will detail how to transition over to the Keto diet without any side affects. Then you will have three separate 7 day meal plans to choose from so that you can jump start your weight loss journey!

Chapter 1: Ketogenic Diet and the Simple Science Behind It

Let's now head back to 6th grade science class and take a look at the science behind the Ketogenic diet. There have been hundreds of studies on how the Ketogenic diet encourages weight loss without hindering performance. Check out this case study conducted by the International Society of Sports Nutrition Journal;

> *Eight elite gymnasts between 20 and 26 years old were recruited and were placed on the Ketogenic diet. Body fat and performance tests were taken before and after the diet. The diet consisted of green vegetables, olive oil, fish, and meat, and virtually no carbohydrates.* **After thirty days significant losses were seen in body fat but no difference was noticed in performance.** *It was concluded that a Ketogenic diet is beneficial for weight loss without reducing performance abilities.*

The Ketogenic diet is also known as the low carb diet. When the body is starved of carbohydrates the body is induced into a state of ketosis. Ketosis is just a natural bodily state that is produced usually during survival mode. When the body is starved of carbs, ketones are produced that help to break down body fat and use it as energy. On the Keto diet however instead of actually allowing the body to go into survival mode the diet just tricks it by replacing the usual energy source (carbs) for the new energy source (fats). This diet recommends 65% of calories coming from fats, 30% coming from proteins and 5% coming from complex carbs.

Now let's compare the Keto diet it to a normal diet with an average carbohydrate intake. On a normal carb diet the body produces glucose and insulin. Glucose is the easiest form of molecule for the body to break down and use as energy. So this is the body's first choice when it needs energy. Therefore because glucose is being used as energy, your fat supply is not required. This leaves you with your normal weight.

How Long Until Ketosis

A Ketogenic diet is like a full time job. You can't just quit when you want and then start up again. It takes time for the body to begin the ketosis process. So depending on your body it can take anywhere between 6-8 days for this to happen. So if you accidently have a slice of pizza or other carb rich food your body will need to start the process all over again. That's why when you decide to begin the Ketogenic diet you have to be dedicated 100%. No cheat meals, no wedding cake and no Nutella. However just like a full time job, if you can dedicate yourself to this diet it will reward you in the long term.

The quickest way to get your body beginning the ketosis process is by drinking a lot of water, eating exactly what you are meant to, restricting your carb intake to 20-25g per day and exercising regularly and if possible on an empty stomach. This will help your body start Ketosis a lot quicker than normal.

How to Tell if You are in Ketosis

The easiest way to find out if your body is in Ketosis is to use a Ketostix. All you have to do is pee on the stick and it will indicate if your body is or is not in Ketosis. These can be purchased at most pharmacies. However they are known to be inaccurate so just be aware of this. If the stick turns pink or purple, that means ketones are being produced in your body. The Ketostix measures the amount of acetone in your urine.

However if you want a more reliable source then the only way to measure your ketone level is by using a blood ketone meter. It is however more invasive and expensive. You need to prick yourself and then place it on the meter for it to read your levels.

For those who do not want to do use either of these methods, there are a number of symptoms that could indicate ketosis. Here is a list:

- Breath that smells fruity or like acetone – like the smell of nail polish or nail polish remover
- Increased rapid breathing or shortness of breath
- Excessive thirst
- Loss of short term memory
- Frequent urination
- Possible stomach pain
- Fatigue, weakness
- Confusion

Remember

When people say 'low carb diet' most people freak out and say that's bad for you and you can get metabolic damage etc. The key thing to remember is that this is a 'diet' not a 'lifestyle'. It should be used only for a certain period of time – no more than 4 months. Then when one has reached their goal weight, a normal diet should begin.

Chapter 2: 10 Benefits of Going on a Ketogenic Diet

There are many benefits to starting a Ketogenic diet. It will not only help you to lose weight but it will also reduce your appetite, reduce the chances of future disease development and increase you energy levels. Here are the top 10 benefits for starting a Keto diet.

1. **Encourages Weight Loss**
   As explained in the section above, when the body is starved of carbs it begins to use the fat stores for energy. This leads to faster weight loss. There is not only fat loss but also water loss. Carbs hold water in the body, so when they are eliminated the kidneys begin to excrete sodium and water.
2. **Increased Good Cholesterol**
   There is good and bad cholesterol. HDL (good) is increased when we eat good fats. This builds up and protects our arteries from blocking.
3. **Disease Prevention**
   The Keto diet reduced blood pressure and bad cholesterol which significantly reduced the risk of developing future diseases.
4. **Increased Energy Levels**
   Energy from fat lasts longer than energy from glucose. People have found that their performance is enhanced when on a Keto diet.
5. **Reduced Hunger**
   Hunger really is the worst aspect of dieting. It is the main reason why so many people fail on their weight loss journeys. So one of the great benefits of eating low carb is that is actually reduces appetite. This does not happen straight away but after around 2 weeks more people say they have to force themselves to eat. A high fat and protein diet causes people to stay fuller for longer and feelings of hunger is reduced.
6. **Can Help Manage Current Illnesses**
   These days people have been turning to natural remedies to cure their illnesses. Many cancer patients or those with diabetes use the Keto diet to fight their sickness.
7. **Reduces Bloating**
   Carbs are heavy on the digestive system, which leads to bloating. So when carbs are replaced with fats and proteins, the digestive system begins to repair itself leading to a flat and healthy stomach.
8. **Reduced Blood Sugar and Insulin Levels**
   Carbs are always broken down in to glucose, which is just sugar. Many people these days have problems with insulin resistance, which leads to different types of diabetes. So by lowering our carb intake diabetes can be prevented or managed.
9. **Reduced Blood Pressure**

High blood pressure can lead to many diseases. Studies show that a low carb diet that is high in protein reduces blood pressure.

10. **Therapeutic for Several Brain Disorders**

    The Keto diet first started as a treatment for epilepsy patients. Now it is used as a method for treating a number if brain disorders. It can help with Epilepsy, Alzheimer's and Parkinson's.

CHAPTER 3: HOW TO MAKE YOUR TRANSITION TO KETOGENIC DIET GO AS SMOOTHLY AS POSSIBLE

You have already made the first step towards transitioning over to the Ketogenic diet, that is by reading this ebook. You first need to fully inform yourself of what this diet is and how it can best be used for you and your goals.

The next step, ladies you are going to like this one, is to go shopping! Get to know which foods you should and should not eat. Learn which foods are high in carbs and which are low in carbs. The same goes for fats and proteins. Here is a shopping list recommended for you:

Meats, Poultry & Seafood:

- Chicken - whole or parts
- Beef steaks and tips
- Bacon, ham and sausage
- Pork loin, chops or steaks
- Pork or beef ribs
- Beef or pork roasts
- Ground beef
- Ground turkey
- Cold cuts such as turkey breast and pastrami (check for added sugars)
- Pepperoni sticks or slices
- Salami and bologna
- Proscuitto
- Fresh or frozen, easy-to-peel shrimp
- Fresh or frozen fish
- Tuna in oil or water
- Fresh or canned salmon
- Fresh or frozen scallops
- Crab

Dairy Products

- Eggs
- Heavy cream
- Sour cream
- Cream cheese
- Butter
- Cheese: hard cheeses such as cheddar and parmesan
- Cheese: soft cheeses such an muenster and farmer
- Greek yogurt, plain, full fat. Carb count should be less than 7 per serving.

Low carb vegetables

- Bell peppers
- Broccoli
- Cucumbers
- Cabbage
- Cauliflower
- Lettuce: large leaves to act as the "bread" for sandwiches
- Leafy green vegetables such as spinach and kale
- Onions and garlic: for flavorful cooking
- Sprouts for salads
- Summer squash such as zucchini

Nuts & Seeds

- Almonds
- Hazelnuts
- Pecans
- Walnuts
- Macadamias
- Sunflower
- Pumpkin
- Sesame seeds
- Avocados
- 100% peanut butter
- 100% almond butter

Low Carb Fruits

- Raspberry

- Blueberries
- Blackberries
- Strawberries

Pantry

- Canned tuna, salmon, crab, shrimp, sardines, anchovies
- Vienna sausages, canned luncheon meat
- Tomato products
- Sauces: Pasta sauce, pizza sauce and alfredo sauce with no added sugar or thickeners
- Canned vegetables: green chiles, roasted red peppers, chipotle peppers, mushrooms, artichoke hearts, sun-dried tomatoes in oil
- Chicken and/or vegetable stock
- Almond milk
- Sugar-free dill pickles or relish: use for tuna or egg salad
- Mustard
- Cider and wine vinegars
- Most bottled hot sauces
- Most salsas
- Tamari soy sauce
- Mayonnaise – look for the brands with the lowest carbs
- Sugar-free salad dressings
- Capers
- Horseradish
- Olives
- Lemon or lime juice

Cooking or Baking Ingredients

- Whey protein powder
- Splenda or other artificial sweeteners or
- Erythritol, xylitol and other sugar alcohol sweeteners
- Herbs and spices
- Extracts (vanilla, lemon, almond, etc.) – avoid the ones with sugar.
- Broth or bouillon
- Cocoa powder which is unsweetened
- Gelatin (plain)
- Xanthan gum for thickening and binding

- Extra-virgin olive oil
- Peanut oil and coconut oil for cooking
- Sesame oil for salad dressings
- Almond flour or other nut flours: flour substitute; keep these in freezer

The next step is to know your intakes – 65% from good fats, 30% from protein and 5% from carbs. Then once you have finished your shopping start to cut carbs slowly. Don't jump to 5% carbs straight away. Just do this progressively over 7 days. Then once you think you are down to 5% it's time to track your macros.

Macro counting is the same as calorie counting except that you know from which nutrients your food is coming from. For example in 100g of chicken breast there is 21g of protein and 172 calories in total. A woman who wants to lose weight should aim to eat around 1600 calories per day and a man aiming to lose weight should aim for 2300 calories per day. Then to track your calories and nutrient intake you will need to use a program like myfitnesspal or fooducate. After a while using a calorie counter app you will just automatically know which foods you should and should not use.

We understand that this can be quite confusing so we have made it easier for you and provided you with three easy to follow 7 day meals plans down below. Feel free to print these meal plans out and follow them daily.

Chapter 4: One-Week Keto Meal Plan #1 (3 meals and 2 snacks daily)

Day 1

1. 3 scrambled eggs, 1 coffee with full cream milk
2. 15 almonds
3. 1 wholegrain wrap with 2 slices turkey breast, lettuce, cheese, 1 tsp mayonnaise, ½ tomato
4. ½ avocado, 2 tbsp cottage cheese, ½ tomato
5. 2 bowls chicken soup, large garden salad with Italiano dressing

Fats	Protein	Carbs	Total Calories
135g	72g	25g	1603

Day 2

1. 3 egg and veggie omelet, 1 coffee with full cream milk
2. 15 walnuts
3. 15 veggie sticks with 2 tbsp cottage cheese, 2 tbsp peanut butter, 2 tbsp spring onion dip
4. 4 small blocks cheese with 5 cherry tomatoes
5. 4 veggie muffins, large garden salad with Italiano dressing

Fats	Protein	Carbs	Total Calories
141g	58g	14g	1557

Day 3

1. Berry smoothie: ½ cup strawberries, ½ cup blueberries, ½ apple
2. 15 almonds
3. 3 veggie muffins
4. 1 avocado with Italiano dressing
5. Rolled Salmon, 1 bowl steamed green veggies

Fats	Protein	Carbs	Total Calories
136g	78g	21g	1620

Day 4

1. 2 scrambled eggs, 1 slice cheese, 1 slice bacon, 1 coffee with full cream milk
2. 10 veggie sticks with 2 tbsp cottage cheese
3. Rolled Salmon, 1 bowl green salad
4. 1 apple
5. Tuna stir fry with bowl broccoli

Fats	Protein	Carbs	Total Calories
135g	91g	22g	1667

Day 5

1. Cottage cheese pancakes, 1 coffee with full cream milk
2. 15 walnuts
3. Mexican burrito
4. 3 celery stalks with 3 tsp peanut butter
5. 2 large San Choy Bow with green salad

Fats	Protein	Carbs	Total Calories
137g	98g	14g	1681

Day 6

1. Banana smoothie: 1 cup almond milk, 1 small banana, 1 tsp cinnamon
2. 1 string cheese
3. 2 large San Choy Bow, 1 garden salad
4. 1 avocado, 2 tbsp cottage cheese
5. 1 serve Chicken Satay, 1 bowl broccoli

Fats	Protein	Carbs	Total Calories
144g	87g	19g	1720

Day 7

1. 2 fried eggs, 1 tbsp cottage cheese, 1 coffee with full cream milk
2. 1 cup strawberries, 6 almonds
3. 1 serve chicken satay, green salad
4. ½ cup blueberries, 6 almonds
5. Ricotta Veggie Stack

Fats	Protein	Carbs	Total Calories
132g	79g	22g	1592

Chapter 5: One-Week Keto Meal Plan #2 (3 meals and 2 snacks daily)

Day 1

1. Tofu and 2 egg scramble, 1 cup coffee with full cream milk
2. 15 almonds
3. Egg salad with 2 slices bacon
4. 1 avocado with salt and pepper
5. 2 stuffed peppers, green salad

Fats	Protein	Carbs	Total Calories
146g	84g	18g	1722

Day 2

1. 2 scrambled eggs with small pork sausage, 1 coffee, with full cream milk
2. 15 almonds
3. 2 stuffed peppers, 1 bowl salad
4. ½ cup cottage cheese, cinnamon
5. 4 tuna patties, 1 bowl steamed green veggies

Fats	Protein	Carbs	Total Calories
148g	72g	25g	1720

Day 3

1. 2 scrambled eggs with 2 slices bacon, 1 coffee with full cream milk
2. 1 cup strawberries
3. 3 tuna patties, 1 bowl green salad
4. 15 walnuts
5. 3 zucchini boats

Fats	Protein	Carbs	Total Calories
128g	76g	19g	1532

Day 4

1. Cottage cheese pancakes, 1 coffee with full cream milk
2. 15 walnuts, 1 apple
3. 3 slice zucchini pizza
4. 1 string cheese
5. 200g salmon steak topped with 2 tbsp cappers, 1 bowl broccoli

Fats	Protein	Carbs	Total Calories
115g	95g	25g	1515

Day 5

1. 3 egg veggie omelet, 1 coffee with full cream milk
2. 1 apple
3. 100g grilled salmon, salad
4. 10 veggie sticks, 2 tbsp cottage cheese
5. Veggie and beef stir fry

Fats	Protein	Carbs	Total Calories
131g	101g	24g	1679

Day 6

1. Superfood smoothie: ½ banana, chia seeds, 6 almonds, 1 cup almond milk
2. 1 cup strawberries, 6 almonds
3. Veggie beef stir fry
4. 3 celery stalks, 3 tsp almond butter
5. 3 slices zucchini pizza, grilled veggies

Fats	Protein	Carbs	Total Calories
122g	91g	31g	1586

Day 7

1. 2 fried eggs, ½ avocado, 1 coffee with full cream milk
2. ½ cup blueberries, 10 almonds
3. Pesto chicken wrap
4. ½ avocado, salt and pepper
5. 2 slices veggie quiche

Fats	Protein	Carbs	Total Calories
133g	89g	25g	1653

Chapter 6: One-Week Keto Meal Plan #3 (3 meals and 2 snacks daily)

Day 1

1. 2 poached eggs, ½ avocado, 2 slice turkey breast, 1 coffee with full cream milk
2. 15 almonds
3. Egg and cucumber salad
4. 100g beef jerky
5. Beef bolognaise over grilled vegetables

Fats	Protein	Carbs	Total Calories
137g	92g	19g	1677

Day 2

1. 2 small blueberry pancakes, 1 coffee with full cream milk
2. ½ avocado
3. Tuna salad
4. 15 walnuts
5. 2 pork sausages, grilled vegetables

Fats	Protein	Carbs	Total Calories
141g	105g	15g	1749

Day 3

1. Breakfast burrito, 1 coffee with full cream milk

2. 15 almonds
3. 2 pork sausages, 1 bowl salad
4. ½ avocado, salt and pepper
5. 2 zucchini pancakes, 1 bowl vegetables

Fats	Protein	Carbs	Total Calories
139g	106g	21g	1759

Day 4

1. Chia overnight pudding, 1 coffee with full cream milk
2. Cucumber salad
3. Egg salad
4. 15 walnuts
5. Chicken parmi with green salad

Fats	Protein	Carbs	Total Calories
139g	101g	12g	1703

Day 5

1. 3 hard boiled eggs, 3 tbsp cottage cheese, 1 coffee with full cream milk
2. 15 almonds
3. BLT wrap
4. 1 apple
5. Chicken stir fry, salad

Fats	Protein	Carbs	Total Calories

138g	102g	22g	1738

Day 6

1. Almond smoothie: 2 tbsp peanut butter, ½ banana, 1 cup almond milk, 1 tsp cinnamon
2. 100g beef jerky
3. Chicken stir fry, salad
4. 15 walnuts
5. 250g steak with mushroom sauce, 1 bowl broccoli

Fats	Protein	Carbs	Total Calories
150g	79g	21g	1750

Day 7

1. Cottage cheese pancakes with 1 tsp peanut butter, 1 coffee with full cream milk
2. 15 almonds
3. 3 egg spinach omelet
4. 1 cup strawberries
5. 2 beef sausages, 1 bowl vegetables

Fats	Protein	Carbs	Total Calories
142g	111g	18g	1794

Recipes:

Tofu scramble

Ingredients:

- 1/2 small red capsicum, finely chopped
- 1/2 white onion, chopped
- 4 mushrooms, diced
- 1 cup baby spinach
- 1 tbsp olive oil
- 1/2 tsp ground coriander
- 2oz blocks extra-firm tofu
- 1 tsps ground turmeric
- Pinch salt, pinch pepper

Method:

- Once drained, smash tofu.
- Heat oil in a fry pan over medium heat. Add onion and capsicum. Then cook, stirring occasionally, until softened.
- Stir in mushrooms, baby spinach, tofu, coriander, and cook until fragrant. Stir in tofu, then turmeric. Season with salt and pepper.

Green Veggie Omelet

Ingredients:

2 eggs

1 egg white

¼ zucchini, grated

½ white onion

1 cup baby spinach

Method:

On low heat, heat a fry pan with a little olive oil. Sauté onions in fry pan and then add zucchini. Once zucchini is soft add the baby spinach until sautéed. Then add the eggs. After 1 minute flip and cook on other side for a further 1 minute.

Chia Pudding

Ingredients:

1 cup milk or soy milk or almond milk

½ cup chia seeds

1 tsp cinnamon

2 tbsp crushed walnuts

Method:

In a cup mix all ingredients together. Then leave the cup in the fridge for 4 hours or overnight until chia absorbs the milk. Serve.

Breakfast Burrito

Ingredients:

1 wholegrain wrap

2 eggs

2 drops Tabasco

1 tbsp coriander

1 tbsp basil

½ red onion

1/3 red capsicum

1 tsp olive oil

Method:
On a low heat, heat a fry pan. Add the chopped capsicum and diced red onion. Once sautéed add the eggs, Tabasco, coriander and basil. Once the eggs are cooked, fold into the wholegrain wrap and serve.

Tofu Veggie Stir Fry: Serves 1
Ingredients:

½ cup brown rice or 2min quick cook brown rice

3 oz hard tofu

1 bag mixed veggies

1 tsp soy sauce

1 tsp sweet chilli sauce

Method:

Cook the brown rice in a pot of boiling water for around 20 minutes or until soft. Then steam the vegetables on the stove or in the microwave for 20 minutes. Cut the tofu into squares and grill on a fry pan. Then mix all ingredients together in a large bowl and serve.

Egg Veggie Muffins: Serves 8 muffins

Ingredients:

- 8 eggs
- 1 cup diced broccoli
- 1 cup diced onion
- 1 cup diced mushrooms
- 1 cup diced red capsicum
- Salt and pepper, to taste

Method:

- Preheat oven to 400F.
- In a large mixing bowl, whisk together eggs, vegetables, salt, and pepper.
- Pour mixture into a greased muffin pan, the mixture should evenly fill 8 muffin cups.
- Bake 18-20 minutes, or until a toothpick inserted in the middle comes out clean.

Tuna Stir Fry: Serves 1

Ingredients:

½ cup brown rice or 2min quick cook brown rice

1 large can tuna in olive oil blend

1 bag mixed veggies

1 tsp soy sauce

1 tsp sweet chilli sauce

Method:

Cook the brown rice in a pot of boiling water for around 20 minutes or until soft. Then steam the vegetables on the stove or in the microwave for 20 minutes. Drain the can of tuna and then mix all ingredients together in a large bowl.

Vegetable Quiche: Serves 4

Ingredients:

- 1/2 red capsicum, chopped
- 6 broccoli florets, chopped
- 1 small zucchini, chopped
- 1/3 cup fetta cheese, crumbled
- 8 eggs
- 1 teaspoon oil
- Salt and pepper

Method:

- Sautee veggies in oil until tender.

- Beat eggs in bowl, add salt and pepper add veggies, fetta to eggs and mix well.

- Spray glass pie plate with olive oil spray.

- Pour the egg mixture in pie plate.

- Bake at 550F for 15-17 minutes.

Tuna Patties: Serves 4 patties

Ingredients:

- 1 Capsicum, diced
- 1 white onion, chopped
- 1 carrot, grated
- ½ cup almond meal
- 2 X big cans tuna
- 1 egg
- 2 egg whites

Method:

- Simply brown onion and capsicum
- Then mix all ingredients together
- With wet hands shape patties
- Either lightly fry patties on a pan until cooked through (about 5 mins each side) or bake in the oven for on 400F for 15mins each side.

San Choy Bow: Serves 5 lettuce cups

Ingredients:

- 2 tablespoons oil
- 1 medium onion, diced
- 3.5oz tofu
- 2 cloves garlic, diced
- 1 cup red lentils, rinsed until water runs clear
- 8 oz. tin of water chestnuts, diced
- 1 medium sized carrot, diced
- 6 whole shiitake mushrooms, diced
- 1 1/4 cups vegetable stock
- 5 stalks spring onion
- 2 tablespoons light soy sauce
- 2 tablespoons oyster sauce
- 1 whole iceberg lettuce

Method:

- In a large saucepan on medium heat, add 2 tablespoons of oil. Add the onion and garlic until cooked through. Then add the tofu and cook. Add the lentils, water chestnuts, carrot, mushrooms, stock and simmer with lid on for 10 minutes stirring to prevent the lentils from sticking at the bottom. Add the spring onion in the last 5 minutes.

- Add the soy sauce and oyster sauce and stir to combine.

- Take the whole iceberg lettuce and remove any extra leaves on the outside. Remove the core and run cold water down the center of the lettuce and allow to sit for a minute. Peel off lettuce leaves one at a time. Serve the mixture inside the lettuce leaves.

Zucchini Pizza Boats: Serves 4

Ingredients:

- 4 zucchinis
- 6 tbsp tomato based pasta sauce (bought in the supermarket)
- 3oz tofu, thinly sliced
- 2 tbsp grated vegan cheese slices (bought in the health food store or supermarket)
- 1 tbsp oregano
- 4 sliced mushrooms

Method:

- Preheat the oven to 400F
- Cut each zucchini into four long strips
- Line a tray with parchment paper and add the strips
- Top with 1 tbsp pasta sauce, some cheese, mushrooms and tofu.
- Bake for 20 minutes
- Top with oregano and serve

Satay Chicken

Ingredients

- 500g chicken breast, chopped into blocks
- 2 cloves fresh garlic, crushed
- 2 tbs soy sauce
- 2 tsp honey
- 1/4 tsp dried turmeric
- 1 medium fresh lime
- 1 tbs light peanut butter
- 1/3 cup reduced-fat coconut milk

Method

- Combine the chicken, garlic, soy sauce and honey in a glass bowl.
- Preheat oven to 550F/280 degrees, grill.
- Thread chicken onto 4 skewers. Cook for 3 minutes each side or until brown and cooked through.
  Meanwhile, combine the turmeric, lime juice, peanut butter and coconut milk in a small saucepan and bring to a simmer over medium heat. Simmer, stirring, for 3 minutes or until fragrant. Taste and season with salt.

Top the chicken with satay sauce.

Tuna Stir Fry

Ingredients

- 4 spring onions
- 2 celery stalks
- 1 white onion
- 1 large broccoli
- 200g baby spinach
- 1 zucchini
- 300g tuna in olive oil blend
- 2 tbsp oyster sauce
- 2 tbsp sweet chilli sauce
- 2 tbsp low salt soy sauce

Method

Dice the spring onions and celery.

Dice the onion and zucchini.

Cut the chicken into bite size pieces.

Cut the broccoli into bite size pieces.

Saute the onions first and then add the rest of the vegetables.

Lightly fry vegetables and then add all three sauces.

Then add the chicken and grill.

Once chicken is cooked through, serve.

Veggie and Beef Stir Fry

Ingredients

- 4 spring onions
- 2 celery stalks
- 1 white onion
- 1 large broccoli
- 200g baby spinach
- 1 zucchini
- 400g low fat minced beef
- 2 tbsp oyster sauce
- 2 tbsp sweet chilli sauce
- 2 tbsp low salt soy sauce

Method

Dice the spring onions and celery.

Dice the onion and zucchini.

Cut the chicken into bite size pieces.

Cut the broccoli into bite size pieces.

Saute the onions first and then add the rest of the vegetables.

Lightly fry vegetables and then add all three sauces.

Then add the mince and fry.

Once beef is cooked through, serve.

Chicken Stir Fry

Ingredients

- 4 spring onions
- 2 celery stalks
- 1 white onion
- 1 large broccoli
- 200g baby spinach
- 1 zucchini
- 400g chicken breast
- 2 tbsp oyster sauce
- 2 tbsp sweet chilli sauce
- 2 tbsp low salt soy sauce

Method

Dice the spring onions and celery.

Dice the onion and zucchini.

Cut the chicken into bite size pieces.

Cut the broccoli into bite size pieces.

Saute the onions first and then add the rest of the vegetables.

Lightly fry vegetables and then add all three sauces.

Then add the chicken and fry.

Once chicken is cooked through, serve. Stuffed Peppers

Ingredients

- 1 cup dried soy meat
- 1 large onion, diced
- 2 cloves garlic, grated
- 1/2 medium lemon, juiced and zested

- 4 medium mushrooms, diced
- 1 medium tomato, diced
- 1/3 can corn
- 100g/3.5oz feta, crumbled
- 1/4 cup pine nuts
- 1/2 cup fresh oregano, parsley and chives
- Salt and pepper
- 4 red capsicums
- 400g low fat minced beef

Method

Carefully remove the top of your capsicum and scrape out the inside seeds and ribs.

In a pot lightly sauté all the vegetables and then add the minced beef. Let is simmer for 15 minutes until beef is well cooked.

Then spoon filling into capsicum and bake at 200C for about 45 minutes, or until capsicum is cooked through. Serve.

<u>Bolognese</u>

Ingredients

- 2 tbsp Olive Oil
- 500g/17oz extra lean minced beef
- 1 onion, diced
- 2 tbsp crushed minced garlic
- 2 tbsp tomato paste
- 1 jar reduced salt pasta sauce
- 1 can diced tomatoes
- 1 cup sliced mushrooms
- 1 tsp Italian mixed herbs
- 2 small zucchinis, grated
- 1 carrot, grated
- 3 tbsp parsley, chopped
- 1/2 punnet cherry tomatoes, halved

Method

In a frying pan, pour in the olive oil and fry onion until soft. Then add minced beef until browned.

Add garlic, tomato paste and fry for a further 2 minutes.

Add pasta sauce, mushrooms, carrot, zucchini and herb mix. Cover and simmer for 20 minutes.

Then stir through cherry tomatoes.

Chicken Soup

Ingredients

- 1 tbsp olive oil
- 2 carrots, peeled, diced
- 300g shredded chicken breast
- 2 zucchini, diced
- ½ cup pea
- 2 sticks celery, diced
- 1 white onion, finely chopped
- 400g diced tomatoes
- 2 cups Reduced Salt Vegetable Stock
- 1 cup water
- 1/2 cup flat-leaf parsley leaves, chopped

Method

Heat oil in a large saucepan on medium heat.

Add carrots, chicken, zucchini, peas, celery and onion. Cook, stirring occasionally, until vegetables begin to soften.

Then add tomatoes, water and stock to pan. Cover with lid and bring to boil. Reduce heat to low. Let simmer, partially covered, for around 15 minutes unti vegetables are soft.

Sprinkle with parsley and serve with lemon wedges.

<u>Zucchini Pizza topped with Chicken and Veggies</u>

Ingredients

Zucchini Crust

- 8 cups shredded zucchini
- 2/3 cup almond flour
- 2 cloves garlic, grated
- 3 tsp dried oregano
- 1 tsp basil
- 2 eggs, beaten
- 1/2 tsp salt

Pizza Topping

- Pasta Sauce
- 100g/3.5oz chicken, cubed
- ½ red onion
- 1 red capsicum, chopped

Method

<u>Zucchini Pizza Crust</u>

- Preheat oven to 550F/280 degrees
- In a large bowl, toss the zucchini with 1 teaspoon coarse salt and set aside for 15 minutes. Squeeze the excess moisture out of the mix by wrapping it up in a clean tea towel or piece of cheese cloth and wringing it out, throw out the water.
- Place the shredded zucchini back into the bowl and add the almond meal, garlic, oregano, basil, eggs, and salt.
- With your hands, mix.
- Place the zucchini mixture onto a piece of parchment paper at least 15" in diameter, set on something solid that will make it easy to transfer into the oven.

- Using your fingers, spread the zucchini crust mixture to form a circle about 1/2" thick. Pinch the edges up so that it forms a nice crust.
- Once the pizza crust has been shaped, place in the oven and bake for 8 minutes or until the crust starts to brown.
- Take pizza out and top the pizza with pasta sauce, chicken cubes and vegetables.
- Place the pizza back in the oven and cook for a further 15-20 minutes.

Rolled Salmon

Ingredients

- 3 large eggplants, cut into thin slices
- Ricotta
- Red capsicum, cut long
- Smoked salmon
- 1 tsp oregano
- 1 tsp basil
- 4 mushrooms
- 2 tsp olive oil
- Tooth picks

Method

Preheat the oven to 550F/280 degrees.

On a tray spread out olive oil.

In a bowl mix in all ingredients except eggplant.

Lay out eggplant flat on the olive oil lined tray. Scoop about a handful of the mix onto the eggplant and then roll the eggplant around the max and put a toothpick through it to hold.

Spray olive oil onto eggplants and bake in the over from 15-20 minutes.

Turkey Burgers

Ingredients

- 1 red capsicum, chopped
- 1 white onion, diced
- 3 carrots, grated
- 100g Almond meal
- 300g low fat minced turkey
- 3 eggs

Method

Dice capsicum and onion.

Then simply sauté onions and capsicums

Then mix all ingredients together in a large mixing bowl.

Then with hands need the mixture into burgers.

Then with minimal olive oil, fry lightly on a pan.

Fry each side for around 3 minutes.

Cottage Cheese Pancakes

Ingredients

- ½ cup cottage cheese
- 1 egg
- 3 tablespoons almond flour
- ½ teaspoon baking powder

Method

- Whisk together all ingredients until smooth.
- If batter looks too runny for your liking, add more almond flour. It should be an easily pourable consistency, but not super runny.
- Then in a non-stick fry pan pour in batter on medium heat.
- Once mixture starts to bubble flip it over for a further 2 minutes.
- Serve while hot.

Pesto Chicken Wrap

Ingredients:

- 1 tsp pesto sauce
- 100g chicken breast
- Lettuce
- ½ Avocado
- Cucumber
- 1 wholegrain wrap

Method:

- Grill chicken breast until brown and cooked through.
- Spread avocado and pesto onto the wholegrain wrap.
- Then add the chicken, lettuce and cucumber.

Fold and eat or pack for lunch.

Zucchini Pancakes

Ingredients:

- 3 cups zucchini, grated
- 2 cups spring onions, chopped
- 4 eggs, lightly beaten
- ½ cup almond meal
- ⅓ cup chopped fresh thyme or dill
- ½ cup chopped fresh parsley
- ½ tsp. salt
- ½ tsp. ground pepper
- 200g crumbled goats feta cheese
- ½ cup chopped walnuts

Method:

- Place grated zucchini in colander. Sprinkle zucchini with salt and let sit for 30 minutes to drain. Squeeze zucchini between hands to remove liquid or squeeze with a cheese cloth. Then let sit for another 10 minutes.
- Combine zucchini, chopped spring onions, eggs, flour, chopped herbs, salt and pepper in medium bowl. Mix well.
- Mix in the cheese and walnuts into zucchini mixture.
- Then add olive oil to a non-stick frying pan that is on medium heat. Working in batches, drop zucchini mixture into pan using a large spoon. Spread mix into circle shape and then fry until pancakes are golden brown and cooked through, about 3 minutes per side. Then serve topped with some Tzatziki.

Chicken Parmi

Ingredients:

- 3 X large chicken breasts
- 100g almond meal
- 2 X whole eggs
- 1 tbsp oregano
- 1 tbsp rosemary

Method:

- Slice chicken breasts into schnitzel pieces.
- Wisk eggs and dip chicken into mixture
- On a large plate spread almond meal with herbs.
- Then coat the chicken in almond meal with herbs.
- Place a fry pan on medium heat.
- Once hot add 2 tbsp olive oil

Lightly fry coated chicken breast until each side is browned and chicken is cooked through.

BLT Wrap

Ingredients:

- 1 tsp mayonnaise
- 2 large bacon slices
- Lettuce

- 2 slices tomato
- Cucumber
- 1 wholegrain wrap

Method:

- In a fry pan fry the bacon until cooked through
- Spread the mayonnaise on the wholegrain wrap.
- Then add the bacon, lettuce cucumber and tomato.
- Fold and eat or pack for lunch.

Steak with Mushroom Sauce

Ingredients

- 250g steak of your choice
- 1/4 cup butter
- 1 cup mushrooms, sliced
- 1 teaspoon soy sauce
- 3/4 cup heavy cream
- ½ white onion, diced
- 1 tablespoon Dijon mustard
- 1 tablespoon fresh parsley
- Pinch salt and pepper

Method

- Saute the white onion in a small pot until clear.
- Then melt the butter in the same pot.
- Then add the mushrooms until tender.
- Stir in the soy sauce, cream and mustard.
- Bring to a slow boil on medium heat
- Continue to cook until the sauce has thickened. Remember to stir frequently. Then add parsley, salt and pepper.
- On a fry pan or grill, grill the steam until cooked to your liking.

Then pour sauce over the top and serve.

Ricotta Veggie Stack

Ingredients:

- 2 large eggplant, sliced
- 1 red capsicum, sliced
- 2 zucchini, sliced
- 4 mushrooms, sliced
- Salt and pepper
- 2 cups ricotta, crumbled

Method:

- Preheat oven to 550F/280D. Spray a pan with oil spray. Sprinkle the eggplant, capsicum, zucchini and mushrooms with salt and cracked black pepper and spray with oil spray.
- Grill, in batches, until charred and soft.
- Stack the veggies one on top of the other and divide with a layer of ricotta cheese.
- Drizzle each stack with a little olive oil and balsamic vinegar.
- Top with coriander and serve.

Chapter 7: Importance of Proper Hydration

Water is the body's most vital element and therefore it must always be replenished. Water is the most important ingredient in any weight loss journey. Just like you wash an apple in water you should also wash your insides with water. A minimum of 2L (8 glasses) of water a day is generally recommended but if are exercising 3L a day is better. Water aids the digestive system and flushes out sodium, which is the leading cause of bloating and water retention. When the brain is dehydrated it will mistake this feeling for the feeling of hunger, leading you to eat more than usual. Dehydration also leads to lethargy, increased sleep, weakness and ultimately illnesses.

So make sure you keep a bottle of water next to your bed, on your office desk and in your gym bag. Here are some of the key benefits to drinking water:

- Quickens the ketosis process.
- Water helps the body to digest fiber, which is a key nutrient in aiding weight loss and detoxification.
- Water improves our digestive and nutrient absorption functions.
- Water aids in kidney and liver function.
- Water flushes away the toxins that we ingest during the day.
- Dehydration slows down the metabolism, so drinking a sufficient amount of water is required for it to work accurately.
- Water is key to maintaining the oxygen levels in our blood stream so without it we are left feeling tired.
- Water lubricates our joints and reduces muscle soreness.
- Water lowers our calorie intake as it has no calories.
- Water helps our bodies to maintain a healthy and regular bowl movement.

Flavoring your water is a great way to add taste to your water, so here is a quick and easy recipe: In 3L of water add 5 chopped strawberries, 4 crushed mint leaves and squeeze in half a lemon. Leave in the fridge overnight and the next day you will have a refreshing and cold drink to hydrate you throughout the day.

Chapter 8: Transitioning off of Keto Diet to Long-Term Healthy eating

As the name suggests, the Ketogenic diet is only a diet not a lifestyle. This diet should only be used for a certain amount of time and then a normal diet should resume. Carbs are a normal part of the human diet and therefore should not be cut out forever. Once a person has reached their weight loss goal, carbs should slowly be introduced again. Studies have actually found that after around 5 to 6 months on a Keto diet the body starts to plateau. This happens because the body becomes accustom to the diet. So to stop the chances of a plateau your diet always needs to be changing to keep the body predicting.

Here are some tips on how to slowly transition off the Keto diet and onto a healthy eating lifestyle.

Tip 1: Mentally prepare for the transition

After a prolonged period of dieting the mind creates a routine and habits to get through the days. Now that you need to come off the diet most people's initial instinct will be to binge, because they maybe missed pasta or potatoes or lasagna. Whatever you do don't let this happen! The key to not going crazy is to still keep strict and slowly introduce carbs.

Tip 2: Do it slowly

It's time to reintroduce carbs back into your diet. And the best way to do this is gradually. Gradually start to eat only 5 extra grams of net carbs every 7 days. This way you won't automatically bloat or feel inclined to binge. The key to doing this successfully is by planning for the transition.

Tip 3: Create a game plan

You need to plan ahead. Sit down on your own or with a nutriticnist and figure out your game plan. Create some meal plans for the next few weeks that shows exactly what you are going to eat. Try to keep your calories the same but just change your macros. Begin like this:

Week 1: 60% fats, 30% protein, 10% carbs

Week 2: 55% fats, 30% protein, 15% carbs

Week 3: 50% fats, 35% protein, 15% carbs

Week 4: 45% fats, 35% protein, 20% carbs

Tip 4: Work towards a new goal

Because you have already achieved your weight loss goal what next? Most people struggle to make a transition because they don't have a goal anymore. What should they aim for? What do they want? It's very important to set yourself a new goal so that you don't just fall back into your old lazy routine. Maybe you want to build more muscle? Compete in a marathon? Develop abs? Find a new goal and work towards it.

CHAPTER 9: TOP 10 TIPS FOR STAYING ON A KETO DIET

1. **Exercise, Exercise, Exercise!**
   If you want to lose weight quickly, then include exercise in your daily routine. The Keto diet along with exercise will speed up your metabolism like crazy. Within 2 weeks you will see results.

2. **Get Creative**
   Chicken & broccoli, chicken & broccoli, chicken & broccoli, DO NOT just keep eating the same old boring meals. Be creative with your recipes. Make dessert, eat sweats, eat fatty. Try pigs in a blanket, chia pudding, cottage cheese pancakes etc. If you are not the creative type then jump online where there are heaps of fun recipes.

3. **Don't Beat Yourself Up**
   If you accidentally ate that pizza or if a cake accidentally fell into your mouth, don't beat yourself up. Just keep making goals and striving to keep them. The more times you do something, the more it becomes a routine, the more it turns into a habit.

4. **Keep a Journal**
   Make sure you track your progress. This is very important as a journal can show you why you are falling behind or are putting on weight. A journal can also make you feel good if you accomplish an extended period without carbs.

5. **Track Your Macros**
   This is very important to achieve success. You need to watch everything you eat. This will help you to stay on track. Plus you might even be able to fit in dessert every now and then.

6. **You Don't Always Need to Eat Clean**
   The Keto diet is not about eating clean. This diet is awesome because you can eat butter, bacon and cheese. So eat dirty every now and then. Enjoy what you eat and you will forget you are even on a diet.

7. **There is No Such Thing As Too Much Water**
   Water is going to help you to lose weight. It will flush out toxins and aid your digestive system. It will also excrete the sodium in your body that is causing water retention.

8. **Do it With a Friend**
   A diet is always easier when there is someone else doing it with you. So rope in a friend and help each other to smash goals.

9. **Cut the Alcohol**
   Alcohol encourages the storage of fat. So it's best to just drop it all together. Don't worry it's not forever. Reach your weight loss goal and then you can celebrate with a glass of wine or two.

10. **Sleeeeep**

Sleep is very important for the digestive system. This period of rest allows your body to absorb and process everything you ate during the day. So make sure to get at least 7 to 8 hours of sleep each night.

CHAPTER 10: CONCLUSION/FINAL MOTIVATIONAL WORDS

So do you think you are ready to jump start your weight loss journey with the Ketogenic Diet? We think you are! You are now a Keto diet expert so there is nothing to stop you from starting your journey to becoming the best you! The best way to start is to pick a day, write it in your diary, mentally prepare for it and then when that day comes start your journey. Thousands of people have had incredible results with the Keto diet and you can too.

It's time to say goodbye and it's time for you to head to the shops and stock up on that shopping list.

Just remember this – consistency is the key! As long as you are consistent, the results will follow!

Printed in Great Britain
by Amazon